UNANSWERED PRAYER

by

GW00686361

G.D.Bu

1998

Gospel Standard Trust Publications
12 (b) Roundwood Lane
Harpenden
Herts
AL5 3DD

ISBN 1 897837 16 X

Cover Picture: Llyn Gwynant, Snowdonia
(Andy Williams)

Printed by RomFlair Press SRL
Romania

Contents

Preface

The following treatise is sent forth in the prayerful hope that it may be of a little help to some of the Lord's people, who for one reason or another, have to say with Jeremiah, "Also when I cry and shout, He shutteth out my prayer" (Lamentations 3. 8). It does not profess to give all the answers. In truth only the God who searches the heart of man really settles these matters in the souls of His people, but if these few thoughts are used to help one of the Lord's praying yet waiting people it would be a great mercy.

An appendix gives the substance of three letters on prayer by the late Mr F.Windridge written to his wife. These were originally published in the Friendly Companion in 1984.

G.D.Buss

August 1998

UNANSWERED PRAYER

Introduction

"Prayer is an offering up of our desires unto God, for things agreeable to His will, in the name of Christ, with confession of our sins, and thankful acknowledgement of His mercies." Shorter Catechism

The gift of prayer is one of the most precious, and vital, of all the mercies that God has freely granted to His people. From the days of Abel, when, undoubtedly, he would have mingled prayer with his acceptable sacrifice, and when men began to call on the name of the Lord, as recorded in Genesis 4. 26, the Lord has been pleased to hear and answer the cries of sinners, as they have approached Him with their wants and requests. To know the true meaning of the poet's words:

> "Prayer is the soul's sincere desire,
> Uttered or unexpressed;
> The motion of a hidden fire,
> That trembles in the breast," (James Montgomery)

is to walk in the path of the children of God, as they have done throughout the history of this world.

To realise, also, that the Lord Jesus Christ, the dear incarnate Son of God, is not just the only Way to God, through His Name, merits and blood, but, that He Himself, 'trod the path of prayer', is one precious part of the word, *fellowship*, which should make this exercise truly attractive to a spiritually healthy child of God. William Tiptaft once said, "I would not think lightly of that man's religion, who gets answers to prayer."

5

Truly to pray is to be under the divine teachings of the Holy Ghost, for we are so ignorant in this great matter, that, "... we know not what we should pray for as we ought: but the Spirit itself maketh intercession for us with groanings which cannot be uttered" (Romans 8. 26).

What a dreary place this world would be, if there were no prayers permitted to our God, and no spirit of prayer given by Him!

> "That were a grief I could not bear,
> Didst Thou not hear and answer prayer;
> But a prayer-hearing, answering God,
> Supports me under every load." (William Cowper)

Yet, it has to be said, that the perplexity of *unanswered prayer* is one which tests the believing child of God many times in his life of faith. The language of the following Scriptures gives potent force to this fact.

"Will the Lord cast off for ever? and will He be favourable no more? Is His mercy clean gone for ever? Doth His promise fail for evermore? Hath God forgotten to be gracious? Hath He in anger shut up His tender mercies? Selah" (Psalm 77. 7-9).

"Also when I cry out and shout, He shutteth out my prayer" (Lamentations 3. 8).

"Thou hast covered Thyself with a cloud, that our prayer should not pass through" (Lamentations 3. 44).

"For this thing I besought the Lord thrice, that it might depart from me" (2 Corinthians 12. 8).

The complaint of Peter after his fruitless night of fishing is often the same with the Lord's people in this path.

"...Master, we have toiled all the night, and have taken nothing:..." (Luke 5. 5).

6

This little treatise is an attempt to draw some conclusions as to why these complaints should be so common among the people of God, and we hope they may, under God's blessing, be a help to some of His people, who are faced with this perplexity.

WHY IS PRAYER ANSWERED?

In reality, every prayer receives one of the following four answers from God:

(1).   *Yes*. "...be it unto thee even as thou wilt" (Matthew 15. 28).

(2).   *Yes, but not in the way you expect*. "Lord, if Thou hadst been here, my brother had not died." "...Said I not unto thee, that, if thou wouldest believe, thou shouldest see the glory of God?" (John 11. 21, 40).

(3).   *Not yet*. "For ye have need of patience, that, after ye have done the will of God, ye might receive the promise. For yet a little while, and He that shall come will come, and will not tarry" (Hebrews 10. 36-37).

(4).   *No*. "...Father, if Thou be willing, remove this cup from Me: nevertheless not My will, but Thine, be done" (Luke 22. 42).

There are three reasons why prayer is answered:

(1).   *For the sake of Jesus*, "...Whatsoever ye shall ask the Father in My name, He will give it you," (John 16. 23).

(2).   *For the honour and glory of God*, "I love the LORD, because He hath heard my voice and my supplications" (Psalm 116. 1). "O magnify the LORD with me, and let us exalt His

7

name together. I sought the LORD, and He heard me, and delivered me from all my fears" (Psalm 34. 3-4).

(3). *For the good of His people,* "Yea, the LORD shall give that which is good; and our land shall yield her increase" (Psalm 85. 12). "...the LORD will give grace and glory: no good thing will He withhold from them that walk uprightly" (Psalm 84. 11).

WHY ARE SOME PRAYERS NOT ANSWERED?

Before addressing this very real perplexity, it is salutary for us first to remember that often our needs are not met because we neglect to pray.

"...yet ye have not, because ye ask not" (James 4. 2).

> "Oh, what peace we often forfeit!
> Oh, what needless pain we bear!
> All because we do not carry
> Everything to God in prayer."   (Joseph Scriven)

Sometimes, God's children act perversely like Ahaz, "...I will not ask, neither will I tempt the Lord" (Isaiah 7. 12). In other words, he limited the Lord in the same way that Israel limited God, when the spies brought back their report from Canaan. Paul said of them, "So we see that they could not enter in because of unbelief" (Hebrews 3. 19).

We are far more ready to talk about our troubles, than to pray about them.

> "Were half the breath, thus vainly spent
> To heaven in supplication sent,

Your cheerful song would oftener be,
'Hear what the Lord has done for me'". (William Cowper)

Many years ago, a young woman was riding in a lonely spot, on horseback near to the village in which she lived. As she travelled along she heard the voice of a man behind her at some distance, who appeared to be talking to someone, but she could not see who it was. She hid herself behind some trees and as the man passed on horseback, she recognised him as the deacon of a place of worship in her village. As he passed she heard him say, "Oh Lord, do have mercy on the young people living in this village." As he passed on, these words rivetted the mind of this young lady. To think that here was a man, who was not only concerned about his own soul's salvation, but the souls of others, her's included, whilst she had never once prayed about her own soul! This caused such serious reflection that she began to pray, for the first time, for her soul's salvation and in due time the Lord was pleased to bring her to Himself, as a sinner looking for mercy through the blood of Jesus. It was said that, her call by grace was the means of many others in that village being wrought upon by the Holy Spirit in a saving way, rather like the case of the woman of Samaria in John 4.

However the greatest cause of exercise to the Lord's children is often that though they do pray yet apparently there seems to be no answer. For this there may be one of several reasons.

(1) We do not need an answer, because it is already revealed to us in God's Word.

The words of the prophet in Micah 6. 8 are very apposite in considering this aspect of unanswered prayer. "He hath shewed thee, O man, what is good; and what doth the Lord require of thee, but to do justly, and to love mercy, and to walk humbly with thy God?"

The things that are clearly revealed in the Word are an infallible guide to the Lord's people. Often like Philip we ask for something clearer and the loving reproof in John 14. 9 is needed, "...Have I been so long time with you, and yet hast thou not known me Philip?"

Further, we should not need to ask what the Lord's will is concerning leaving a sinful path. An awakened conscience will know that the way is clear. "But thou, O man of God flee these things; and follow after righteousness, godliness, faith, love, patience, meekness" (1 Timothy 6. 11).

The following extract, from the Memoirs and Letters of J.C.Philpot, gives eloquent and adequate testimony to this very important principle.

This extract is from a sermon on Psalm 91. 15 entitled, 'Prayer and its Answer'.

"Now there is sometimes in men's minds a kind of confusion in this matter. They are in a certain path, from which they want to be extricated; they are under a trial, from which they want to be delivered; they call upon the Lord to deliver them; and they ask some manifestation of Himself; some going forth of His hand, some divine leading which they are to follow. But the Lord may be working in a very different way from what they think; and they may really be inattentive to the internal voice of God in their conscience, because they are expecting the voice to come in some other way. It was just so with myself.

When I was in the Establishment, burdened with all the things I had to go through, and troubled and distressed in my mind, I was calling upon the Lord to deliver me, to lead me out, to show me what to do, to make the path plain and clear. Now that was my sincere cry; but I expected some miraculous interposition - to hear some voice, to have some wonderful leading; and in waiting for that, I was waiting for what the Lord never meant to bestow. And I was brought at last to this internal conviction: suppose I were living in drunkenness, suppose I were living in adultery, suppose I were walking in known sin, should I want a voice from God to say to me, 'Leave this drunkenness, come out from this adultery, give up this sin?' Should I want some divine manifestation to bring me out of a sin, when my conscience bore its solemn witness, and I was miserable under the weight and burden of it? No; the very conviction is the answer of God to the prayer; the very burden which the Lord lays on us is meant to press us out of that in which we are walking. So I reasoned with myself: 'If I am living in sin, if it be a sin to be where I am, if I must do things which my conscience tells me are sins, and by which my conscience is burdened as sins, the very conviction, the very distress, the very burden, is the answer. It is the voice of God in the conscience, not the voice of God in the air, not the appearance of God in the sky, but the voice of God in the conscience, and the appearance of the frown of God in the heart.' And on this simple conviction I was enabled to act, and never to this day have repented it. I have, therefore, been led to see by experience, that we are often expecting wonderful answers, mysterious answers, and the Lord does not mean to give those answers."

(2) Because there is some secret evil which God will not disregard, but which we are not made willing to part with or acknowledge.

"If I regard iniquity in my heart, the Lord will not hear me:" (Psalm 66. 18).

When Achan sinned, Israel fell before their enemies. "Israel hath sinned, and they have also transgressed my covenant which I commanded them:...neither will I be with you any more, except ye destroy the accursed from among you" (Joshua 7. 11-12).

For the same reason, as recorded in Jonah 1, it was only when the sailors prayed to the one true God, and cast rebellious Jonah out of the boat that the sea ceased its raging, not before.

Similarly, Samson fell before the Philistines because he had revealed the secret of his strength to Delilah, and his hair was shorn. Significantly, it was when his hair grew again in the prison, that his dying prayer, "...O Lord God remember me, I pray Thee, and strengthen me, I pray Thee, only this once..." (Judges 16. 28), was remarkably answered.

Esau's case is most instructive for more than one reason. He had despised his birthright and now reaped the solemn consequences of exclusion from the blessing. His tears of natural but not spiritual sorrow, were ineffectual in getting Isaac to change his words to Jacob. But what a solemn example this also is, of one who, having sinned against light and knowledge in despising all that the birthright contained, with reference to the coming Messiah, found himself excluded from its deepest blessings.

Further how one thief on the cross angrily confronts the dying Saviour, "...If Thou be Christ, save Thyself and us" (Luke 23. 39). This prayer received no answer, whilst the other dying thief, in humble faith, cries, "...Lord, remember me when Thou comest into Thy kingdom" (Luke 23. 42). Because his heart was right in the sight of God, this simple, yet profound plea found a ready answer from the lips of the Redeemer.

Another prevalent sin which hinders the prayers of God's people is an unforgiving spirit. Twice in the Sermon on the Mount, the Lord Jesus makes mention of this important point.

"Therefore if thou bring thy gift to the altar, and there rememberest that thy brother hath ought against thee; leave there thy gift before the altar, and go thy way; first be reconciled to thy brother, and then come and offer thy gift" (Matthew 5. 23-24).

"For if ye forgive men their trespasses, your heavenly Father will also forgive you: but if ye forgive not men their trespasses, neither will your Father forgive your trespasses" (Matthew 6. 14, 15). In this sense, the Lord's prayer needs much more grace to pray than is often realised, and many inwardly stumble when they reach the words, "Forgive us our debts, as we forgive our debtors" (Matthew 6. 12).

When was it that the captivity of Job was turned? It was when he prayed for his friends as in Job 42. 10.

(3)   We do not ask in faith.

"If any of you lack wisdom, let him ask of God, that giveth to all men liberally, and upraideth not; and it shall be given him. But let him ask in faith, nothing wavering. For he that wavereth is like a wave of the sea driven with the wind and tossed. For let not that man think that he shall receive anything of the Lord" (James 1. 5-7).

By its very nature faith goes hand in hand with sincerity. Where the one is lacking so inevitably is the other.

The words of the children's hymn are very apposite in this connection.

> "I often say my prayers,
> But do I ever pray?
> And do the wishes of my heart
> Go with the words I say?

13

Unanswered Prayer

I may as well kneel down
And worship gods of stone
As offer to the living God
A prayer of words alone.

For words without the heart
The Lord will never hear;
Nor will He to those lips attend
Whose prayers are not sincere.

Lord, teach me what I need,
And teach me how to pray;
Nor let me ask Thee for Thy grace
Not feeling what I say."

(John Burton)

"And all things, whatsover ye shall ask in prayer, believing, ye shall receive" (Matthew 21. 22).

The story is told of a poor old man, who when a child of three years of age, had been taught by his mother to repeat a prayer every night, which he did till he was seventy-three years old; and not a little proud was he to say, that he had not omitted saying his prayers every night for seventy years! At this advanced age it pleased God to afflict him severely; he was led by the Holy Spirit to see that he was a poor sinner who had been living in a form of godliness, but had never felt its power. He was enabled to spend the last few years of his life in humble dependence on the grace of Christ; and when he referred to himself, he would often add, 'I am the old man who said his prayers for seventy years, and yet all that time never prayed at all.'

It is in godly sincerity that, "Out of the abundance of the

heart the mouth speaketh" (Matthew 12. 34), that prayer is received and answered. Much self examination is needed to test the sincerity of our desires.

Many years ago, a young family were on holiday. They had saved up hard to be able to take this break, but while they were away, their car developed serious mechanical problems which resulted in a large and unexpected and unwelcome bill. This couple were obviously greatly distressed, not knowing how to pay this demand. Believing in a God of prayer, the young husband went to the Lord asking for some token that He would come to their aid. No sooner had he prayed in that way, than the Lord lovingly reproved him for his unbelief in seeking a token, when on so many occasions, in times past their needs had been wonderfully met. It was as if the Lord said, 'You don't need a further sign. Have I ever failed you?' By reviewing past mercies this young couple came to the rest of faith in the unchanging character of their God and proved Him to be faithful in meeting this new need in due course.

"His love in times past forbids me to think
He'll leave me at last in trouble to sink;
Each sweet Ebenezer I have in review
Confirms His good pleasure to help me quite through."
(John Newton)

"Delight thyself also in the Lord; and He shall give thee the desires of thine heart" (Psalm 37. 4). It is often a venture of naked faith in Himself, which the Lord delights to honour. Just as in the case of the ten lepers whom our Lord healed. His command was, "Go show yourselves unto the priests. And it came to pass, that, as they went, they were cleansed" (Luke 17. 14).

(4)   We do not ask for the right reasons.

"Ye ask, and receive not, because ye ask amiss, that ye may consume it upon your lusts" (James 4. 3). "...He gave them their request; but sent leanness into their soul" (Psalm 106. 15).

To be like their neighbours, the children of Israel asked for a king. In doing this they rejected God's rule over them, and so we read, "I gave thee a king in Mine anger, and took him away in My wrath" (Hosea 13. 11). How much better it would have been for them to wait for the Lord's time which evidently came, when David was anointed king. In Israel's case, the Lord answered their prayer, - which was uttered for the wrong reasons - in judgment. How we need to be kept and to be guided in our prayers.

So also it was with Job, when he said, "Oh that I might have my request; that God would grant me the thing that I long for." But what was Job's request? Was it for the honour and glory of God? Was it for the good of his soul? No. Job's request to die was not a gracious one and it was in mercy to his soul that the Lord did not answer him. How different was the apostle Paul's language on this point in Philippians 1. 22-23, "For I am in a straight betwixt two, having a desire to depart, and to be with Christ; which is far better: Nevertheless to abide in the flesh is more needful for you."

It is particularly noticeable, how that the Lord, in Matthew 12. 39, rebukes the Pharisees for asking for a sign. "...An evil and adulterous generation seeketh after a sign; and there shall no sign be given to it, but the sign of the prophet Jonas." There was no sign or type needed when the great anti-type, the Lord Jesus was in their midst.

(5)   We do not use the right plea.

The two contrasting features between the prayer of the Pharisee and that of the Publican in Luke 18 are, firstly, that the Pharisee in point of fact only assumed an attitude of prayer, whereas the publican's need of forgiveness was his all-consuming desire.

Secondly, the Pharisee's prayer rested on his own supposed goodness whereas the Publican, feeling to have no righteousness of his own, had only one plea - mercy. It was he who had his prayer answered whereas the Pharisee received nothing, although, solemnly, was probably not even aware that his prayer had not been received, being yet dead in sins.

It was once said that a man once reproved a minister for saying grace in his presence, without mentioning the name of the LORD JESUS CHRIST; and hoped he would be more mindful in future of the apostolic injunction.

(6)   We do not ask according to the will of God.

Many people wrongly think that prayer is a means of obtaining what they want, whereas true prayer is asking according to the will of God. We are prone to ask for things which we do not need. Also to ask for anything which God's word forbids, is an affront to a prayer-hearing and answering God.

"And this is the confidence that we have in Him, that, if we ask any thing according to His will, He heareth us:" (1 John 5. 14).

Yet, how earnestly Moses pleaded to be able to go into the Promised Land, but the LORD said, "...Let it suffice thee; speak no more unto Me of this matter" (Deuteronomy 3. 26). Notice, that it was for the honour and glory of God, that it should be Joshua, whose name means 'saviour', who should lead the children of Israel into Canaan, rather than Moses, who in God's hand, was the giver of the Law. The honour and glory of Christ, in the type, demanded that Moses' prayer should not be answered, as he desired.

In this case, Moses had to walk in the words, "For My thoughts are not your thoughts, neither are your ways My ways, saith the LORD. For as the heavens are higher than the earth, so are My ways higher than your ways, and My thoughts than your thoughts" (Isaiah 55. 8, 9).

Similarly, in Jeremiah, we read, "Therefore pray not thou for this people, neither lift up cry nor prayer for them, neither make intercession to Me: for I will not hear thee" (Jeremiah 7. 16). God's purposes of judgment were fixed against His ancient people on account of their repeated idolatries, and even though Moses and Samuel had been able to intercede for them, the Lord said that His purpose would not be altered (See Jeremiah 15. 1).

Again in Deuteronomy 1. 45 we read these words, after the children of Israel were forbidden to enter Israel because of unbelief, "And ye returned and wept before the LORD; but the LORD would not hearken to your voice, nor give ear unto you."

In their prayers the Lord's people sometimes have to walk in a similar way that Joseph had to walk in a path of self-denial, with respect to the blessing of his two sons. Although Joseph said, "...Not so, my father:..." (Genesis 48. 18) yet the purpose of God, through Jacob's prophecy, was that Ephraim, the younger, should be preferred above Manasseh.

Paul's thorn in the flesh is yet another example. Though he

18

prayed earnestly three times for its removal, yet, it was more for the glory of God and the good of his soul, that it should remain.

Pre-eminently, it was for the greater glory of God, and for the good of the Church, that Christ should drink the cup which His Father gave Him in Gethsemane.

Again, how Paul had to prove that it was not the will of God that he should go either to Asia or Bithynia, but, in answer to the prayers of the women at Philippi, to go to Macedonia.

The example of Martha and Mary, in John 11, is to be commended. When their brother, Lazarus, became sick, they just sent a message to the Lord, "...Lord, behold, he whom Thou lovest is sick" (John 11. 3). They did not tell the Lord what they wanted Him to do: far less did they dictate to Him. They left the whole matter with Him, as David said, "Commit thy way unto the LORD; trust also in Him; and He shall bring it to pass" (Psalm 37. 5).

Some years ago a young child was found by her father playing with razor blades. Although she had already cut herself, when her father took them from her she screamed for them to be given back. Of course the father would not even think of giving in but the child could not understand why. So when God withholds a blessing from us, or takes something away, often we do not understand and in our foolishness persist in asking for it back, when to have it back would be neither for our good nor for the Lord's honour and glory.

"He gives and He takes and He makes no mistakes,
Whatever may be the amount,
Nor have we a right, however He smite,
To ask Him to give an account."

19

It may seem severe, when what is most dear
Is made the first object of call,
Yet made to stand still, we bow to His will,
And own that He's just in it all."

Two experiences in the life of John Warburton as recorded in his "Mercies of a Covenant God," are vivid examples of not asking according to the will of God.

The first occasion was when he thought God was calling him to a pastorate in Yorkshire, and he writes as follows:

About this time I was invited to go and preach at Pool Moor, in Yorkshire, and I believe the Lord went with me, and blessed the word to many of them. My very soul fell in love with the people and the chapel though it stood almost in the midst of a large common. Indeed, I was so taken up with the people and the place that I thought I must die if the Lord would not grant me the situation. I thought that it was just the very spot that God had designed for me, and believed it was the case, because my heart was so knit to it.

At that time the people were without a pastor, and many of them were very fond of me. " O," said I, " it will come to pass in the Lord's own time;" for I was sure that there was nothing impossible with Him, seeing that He had so many times answered my prayers, and had never failed me in all my straits, but had ever been my prayer-hearing and prayer-answering God. So I set to work with all my might to pray for the place. For, thinks I, the Lord says, 'Whatsoever ye shall ask in My Name it shall be given;' and, 'Open thy mouth wide, and I will fill it.' I could bring in plenty of Scriptures if I could but persuade the Lord to perform it in the way that I wanted. And I thought there was no other way but to keep on crying for it night and day; for, thinks I, 'The kingdom of heaven suffereth violence, and the violent take it by force.'

I went several times to supply at this chapel, and every time I went I was more and more in love with the situation. O, thinks I, it is just the very spot for my large family. So again I cried and prayed from week to week; and, to my views at that time, I had such assurances from the Word of God and my own feelings, that I believed at times I was as sure to have it as that there was a God. They had, if I recollect right, Mr. Webster, from Liverpool, to supply a few times, and most of the people were very much attached to him; and, as the time drew on, as I understood that the church intended to give him a call, and some of them expected that it would be done before I came again, they did not, therefore, expect that I should be needed any more after my next journey. But I did not feel much sunk down at this, for I thought that they did not know how many cries and tears I had put up to God. The next Lord's day for my supply was, I think, three weeks from this time, and some of the people hoped it would be my last. And, O, what a three weeks cry I had. It was almost night and day. I shall never forget, at times, when the Saturday came for me to go, what a journey I had of about twenty-two miles. I verily believed, according to my feelings, if it were settled for Mr. Webster to be their pastor that it would kill me.

I arrived in the evening at the house of one of the members, about a mile short of my lodging, and as soon as I got in: "Well, by this time," said I, "I suppose you are settled with a minister, so that I shall not need to toil over any more?" "Why," answers the man, "it was settled for Mr. Webster to come; some of us indeed did not wish it, but numbers overpowered us, and we must submit." O, I thought I must have dropped down in the house. I got my hat, and told the man that I must go. He tried hard to keep me in the house to sit and talk with him; but O no! for if I had not gone out I must have roared out in the house. So out I went, and got into a little valley between two hills, where I believed no soul could hear me, and there I roared out like a raging bear bereaved of her whelps: nay, I had hard work to keep from tearing the very hair from my head. I roared and wept while I had power to weep.

Then the devil set on with all his hellish spleen, and worked up

21

such infidelity in my heart that I never can express a thousandth part of it. "Now," says he, "what do you think of the Bible? Do you think it is true? Have you not prayed for this place hundreds of times, and have not floods of tears flowed from your eyes for it? And does not this Bible say, 'He that soweth in tears shall reap in joy?' but you have sowed in tears and reap in sorrow. And does not the Bible tell you that whatsoever you asked it should be given you? but you have asked, and you believed that you should have the place, and have been denied. There is no God, and the Bible is nothing but priestcraft, and all your preaching and religion is nothing but an empty farce." I roared out again, "O that I could but die! O that I could but sink out of existence!" And such hatred and such awful blasphemies rose up in my heart against God that I felt that, if it were possible, I could have pulled Him from His throne and stamped Him under my feet. O how I struggled till the sweat ran down my wretched face to keep my mouth from uttering what boiled up in my heart!

At last I got to my lodging, but could not sit down, for I was in such a state that I could hardly speak, and my face was foul with weeping. I desired the mistress to give me a candle, and said I would go to bed, for I was very bad. She tried to persuade me all she could that I would let her make something for me that would do me good, but I told her that I wanted nothing but rest; so I took the candle and into my bedroom I went. And the tossings to and fro! sometimes in bed and sometimes walking the room till about four or five o'clock in the morning, till I verily thought that my natural senses were going, and felt quite confident that a mad-house would be my place. But as to pray, to hope, or ever think it possible for me to preach again, I could as soon blot out the sun with my hand as do any of them. But I shall never forget the sound of those words that dropped like rain, and did indeed distil like the dew: "What I do thou knowest not now; but thou shalt know hereafter" (John 13. 7). O the softness these words produced in my heart in a moment! The beasts of the forest all gathered themselves into their dens, my soul sprang up like a bird that had broken out of the snare, and I cried out, "It is the voice of my Beloved." O how my poor soul was melted down at His blessed feet! I covered my shameful face, and could neither look nor speak for wonder and astonishment at what it could all mean. How sweetly did He draw me forth by His blessed words of peace, "Let me see Thy countenance, let me hear Thy voice; for sweet is Thy voice, and Thy countenance is comely" (Solomon's Song 2. 14). My soul was so drawn out and encouraged that I went down on my knees, and felt just like a child. "Lord, how is it, and why is it that my prayers are not answered? O, dear Lord, do show me how it is, and why it is! Thou knowest that I cannot tell how it is, nor why it is! Do, my dear Lord, show Thy poor ignorant, sinful and helpless child: do, my dear Jesus, show me." And O with what light, life, and power did He speak these words into my heart that settled the thing in a moment, and showed me the why and the how: "Ye ask, and receive not, because ye ask amiss, that ye may consume it upon your lusts" (James 4. 3). O how clearly did I see it was all my own fleshly planning and contriving, and that it was to gratify my own fleshly pleasure. O how sweetly could I give it all up into the hands of my covenant God. Never did I go and preach a sermon in my life with more peace and love than my last in Pool Moor Chapel. How I could pray that if it were the Lord's will He would bless them in their choice of a minister. So that what I expected would have been to me nothing but death and destruction was turned into the greatest blessing that I ever had in all my life. O the use I have found it to me hundreds of times since! O the numbers of times I have blessed God for it! But my soul was knit to a few of them, and they were knit to me in love that was never dissolved, and never will be, neither in time or to all eternity.

After a time a few of them separated and took a room, where I went occasionally to supply them for many years, and God owned my poor labours amongst them.

The second occasion in John Warburton's life was relative to his call to the pastorate at Trowbridge, he says:

Unanswered Prayer

A few days after this I received a letter from Maidstone, in Kent, saying that if I was at liberty, they wished me to come for four or six weeks upon trial. I looked upon this as a wonderful opening in providence, and sent them a letter, fixing the time at which I hoped to be there. I think it was the day after I had sent off my answer that I received another letter, from a few people who met in a room at Trowbridge, in Wiltshire, inviting me for a month upon trial, if I was at liberty. O how I wondered to know what all this could mean! I sent them an answer, saying that I would comply with their request as soon as I had fulfilled my engagement at Maidstone. At the time appointed I went to Maidstone, and stayed as long as I had agreed to do.

The people gave me a call to be their pastor, and everything was as pleasant to flesh and blood as I could desire; and fully was I determined to accept the call, only I must go to Trowbridge to fulfil my engagement there. But I was as confident in my own mind that I should come and settle at Maidstone as I was in existence; so to Trowbridge I came to spend my month. The room was crowded with people, and God blessed the word abundantly. But I felt determined I would go to Maidstone.

The people at Trowbridge gave me a call, and, my time being nearly out, it was necessary to give them an answer. O the begging and crying I had that God would give me a command to go to Maidstone! For to pray to stay at Trowbridge I could not; for I could see nothing but difficulties, trials and miseries at Trowbridge; for I plainly saw the toils of a new chapel, and these I dreaded, as knowing what sorrows and miseries Hope Chapel had caused me.

O what a night I had the night before I was to settle the business whether I was to go to Maidstone or stop at Trowbridge. I wrestled and prayed, and cried to God until about three in the morning, to let me go to Maidstone; and O how I sunk down when He spoke these words into my heart: 'Abide in this city, for I have much people here.' "O", cried I, "do, Lord, let me go to Maidstone; do, Lord. Do not be offended with my poor petition; do let me go to

Maidstone." But the text sounded again and again, 'Abide in this city, for I have much people here;' but still I wanted Him to let me go to Maidstone. At last the dear Lord settled the matter at once by speaking these words to my soul:

"If his children forsake My law and walk not in My judgments; if they break My statutes and keep not My commandments; then will I visit their transgression with a rod, and their iniquity with stripes;" and I could see it as speaking all this to my soul: "You may go to Maidstone; but here is the rod, and you shall have nothing else if you go." I fell down and cried out, "Not my will, but Thine be done." " But," cried I, "How can I get on here? How can I live here, when I come with ten in family and my wife in the family way? How can I possibly live here and the people a poor people?" O how God condescended to settle the matter in my soul. 'The cattle upon a thousand hills are Mine.' 'The earth is Mine, and all the gold and silver is Mine.' 'Thy bread shall be given thee, and thy waters shall be sure.' 'Fear thou not; for I am with thee: be not dismayed; for I am thy God: I will strengthen thee; yea, I will help thee; yea, I will uphold thee with the right hand of My righteousness.' I cried out, "It's enough, it's enough: Amen to it." Maidstone from that moment was as completely taken away from my mind, and the feeling of any desire to go there to settle, as if I had never heard of such a place. And here I am at Trowbridge, a poor worm, and have proved the Word of the Lord to be truth for nearly twenty two years.

(7) God's time has not yet come.

Often it is God's sovereign purpose to try His people's faith. For this reason He delayed to give the promised child to Abraham and Sarah. How, in later years Abraham must have regretted his impatience and lack of faith in the matter of Hagar. King Saul many years later proved to be a reprobate character when he forced himself before the Lord, rather than wait for His appearing. On the other hand how the faith of the Syrophenician woman commends itself in its patience, humility and perseverence. If ever a child of God prayed it was in her case. Until the Lord had pronounced the answer she would not let go and what a gracious reward she had, not just the healing of her devil-possessed daughter but the Lord's own testimony concerning the character and nature of her faith. "O woman, great is thy faith: be it unto thee even as thou wilt (Matthew 15. 28).

How, perhaps in the matter of prayer, patience is needed almost as much as any other grace. Consider the following passages.

"...My time is not yet come: but your time is alway ready" (John 7. 6).

"But let patience have her perfect work, that ye may be perfect and entire, wanting nothing" (James 1. 4).

"...Go again seven times" (1 Kings 18. 43).

"Until the time that his word came: the Word of the LORD tried him" (Psalm 105. 19).

"For the vision is yet for an appointed time, but at the end it shall speak, and not lie: though it tarry, wait for it; because it will surely come, it will not tarry" (Habakkuk 2. 3).

"...What I do thou knowest not now; but thou shalt know hereafter" (John 13. 7).

"...till I know what God will do for me" (1 Samuel 22. 3).

The following two extracts confirm this important point. The first is from a book entitled, "A Breathing After God" by the Puritan, Richard Sibbes. In dealing with this question, as to why our prayers are not immediately answered, he writes:

This life is a life of desires. The life of accomplishment is heaven. Then all our desires shall be accomplished, and all pro-

mises performed, and not before then. This is a life of desires, and we must be in a state of desires and prayers still till we be in heaven.

Question: What is the reason that God doth not presently (immediately) accomplish our desires?

Answer: There be diverse reasons.

1. First of all He loves to hear the desires of His servants. He loves to be sued unto, because He knows it is for our good. It is music that best pleaseth God's ears to hear a soul come unto Him to request, especially spiritual things of Him, which He delights most to give, which He knows are most useful and best for us. This pleaseth Him so marvellously that He will not presently (immediately) grant it, but leads us along and along that still He may hear more and more from us.

2. And then to keep us in a perpetual humble subjection and dependence on Him, He grants not all at once, but leads us along by yielding a little and a little, that so He may keep us in humble dependence.

3. And then to exercise all our graces, for a spirit of prayer is a spirit of exercise of all grace. We cannot pray but we must exercise faith, and love to God and His church, and a sanctified judgment to esteem what are the best things to be prayed for, and to exercise mortification. "If I regard sin, God will not regard my prayers." A spirit of prayer is a spirit that puts all into exercise; therefore God, to keep us in the exercise of all grace, answers not at the first.

4. And then He would have us to set a high price upon what we desire and seek after. If we had it at the first, we should not set so high an esteem and price of it.

5. And then, that we might better use it when we have it. Then we use things as we should do when we have gotten them with much ado; when we have won them from God with great importunity, then we keep and preserve them as we should.

These and the like reasons may be given, and you may easily conceive them yourselves. Therefore let us not be offended with

27

God's gracious dispensation if He answer not our desires presently (immediately), but pray still; and if we have the spirit of prayer continued to us, that spirit of prayer is better than the thing we beg a great deal. Ofttimes God answers us in a better kind when He gives us a spirit of prayer, for, increasing a spirit of prayer in us, He increaseth all graces in us. What is it we would have? This or that particular grace? But when God gives us a spirit of prayer, He answers us better than in the thing we ask, for there is all grace. He will answer in one kind or other.

The second extract is from the well-known F. Wilhem Krummacher. In his book, "Elijah the Tishbite", he writes:

When Elijah had wrestled awhile with God in the depth of self-abasement and poverty of spirit in a manner which perhaps few of us know from experience - for all believers do not tread in a path of such a deep and thorough humiliation - he said unto his servant, "Go up now," that is, to the declivity of the mountain. "and look towards the sea!" He placed him as it were on the watch-tower to look out and inform him when his prayer was beginning to be answered by a sign of rain becoming visible in the distant horizon. For he was certain of a favourable answer, in faith on the Word and truth of Him who had said to him at Zarephath, "Go, show thyself to Ahab, and I will send rain upon the earth!"

The servant went, looked out in the distance, and cast his eyes about on all sides; but the sky was as clear as crystal - not a cloud to be seen. He came back, and said, "I see nothing." But it is a matter of daily experience that help does not appear at the first cry, nor is the harvest reaped the moment after the sowing time of prayer. This is certainly not agreeable to flesh and blood, but spiritually considered, it is very salutary. What would be the consequence if God's treasures were always opened to us at our first knocking? Should we not then seem to be rulers and commanders in the city of God and forget our dependent condition? Should we not be in danger of making an idol of our prayer, as the

28

Israelites made of the brazen serpent, and think it is our prayer that effects all, that in it we possess a secret charm, a divining rod or a legal claim upon the bounty of God? We should soon become self-sufficient. Therefore our gracious God does not always appear to hearken to the first cry, but lets us generally stand awhile at the door so that once and again we are obliged to say, "I see nothing." We ought then to reflect a little and become deeply conscious that we have, in reality, nothing to claim, but that all is mere unmerited favour. If we make our first approach to His footstool in the character of just persons, He keeps us back until we feel that we are poor sinners, unworthy petitioners, and are ready to say, "Truth, Lord: yet the dogs eat of the crumbs which fall from their master's table." Such is His method.

"There is nothing," said the servant. But our praying Elijah does not despair. The reason why we generally so easily grow weary, and so soon cease from praying, is because we are not sufficiently in earnest for the blessing we implore. This, however, was not the case with Elijah. He therefore bids the servant to "go again seven times." But why precisely seven times? Does it only mean several times, or is there here any particular emphasis in the number of seven? And why was the servant to go thus again and again? What would it avail him to hear every time, "There is nothing"? Doubtless it stimulated the prophet's ardour, it animated him to wrestle the more earnestly with God, it made him still less and less in his own eyes and drew forth deeper and deeper sighs from his contrite soul. How would his fervour in prayer thus augment from one minute to another! To obtain a speedy hearing is much more agreeable to our natural feelings, but waiting long is far more beneficial for us. Those are the most blessed spots on the face of the, earth where prayer is wont to be made with the greatest fervency and perseverance. During this process of persevering prayer, our corrupt nature receives the most deadly blows. Then is the heart thoroughly broken up and prepared for the good seed of the Word. The remains of self-love are demolished, the chambers of imagery are cleansed, the foundation of truth in the

soul is laid deep, and when at length the answer comes, how great is the joy!

(8)   We are not earnest enough in our prayers.

How rare is Jacob's grace at Peniel, "...I will not let thee go, except Thou bless me" (Genesis 32. 26).
It is most significant that when the church wrestled in prayer for Peter, that he was delivered from the hand of Herod. Did they wrestle for James, I wonder? Also what a value there is in united and importunate prayer in this case! The prayer meeting is often the place in the church's history where the well-known saying has been proved. "There are more things wrought by prayer than this world dreams of."

> "The force of their united cries
> No power can long withstand;
> For Jesus helps them from the skies
> By His almighty hand."
> (John Newton)

Do we know the difference between prayer and supplication? How often we neglect to water our prayers with spiritual tears, we forget what we prayed for, we soon tire and do not look for the answers we professed to need.

.J.C.Philpot made the following comments when preaching from Philippians 4. 6.

But now look at the apostles expression, "by prayer and supplication." We often find these two words united in Scripture. Take the following instances: "Then hear thou from the heavens their prayer and the supplications" (2 Chronicles 6. 39); "I set my face unto the Lord God to seek by prayer and supplications"

(Daniel 9. 3). So our blessed Lord, as our great Examplar, is said, in the days of His flesh, to have offered up "prayers and supplications" (Hebrews 5. 7); and, following His holy example, the eleven disciples, after His ascension, all "continued with one accord in prayer and supplication" (Acts 1. 14). But though thus frequently joined, there is a distinction still to be discerned between them. Prayer comprehends every breathing of the soul, from the feeblest desire, the faintest sigh, and the most tender wish, to the utmost and intensest earnestness, such as Jacob displayed when he wrestled all night with the angel at Peniel. It includes, therefore, all mental prayer and all vocal prayer. Thus, all private prayer, all public prayer, every desire of the heart, all utterance of the mouth, which the blessed Spirit is pleased to raise up by His powerful breath in the soul, or to prompt with the tongue, that we may call, in a scriptural sense, "prayer." Supplication seems to imply something more broken and interrupted; something more poured out with groans and tears and agonising cries. The posture of a suppliant is more humble, his wants more urgent, and his requests more fervent than those of a petitioner. Thus, in the passage which I have already quoted, where our blessed Lord is said to have offered up prayers and supplications, we find added, "with strong crying and tears." When He prayed in calm majesty, as in John 17, that was prayer; when in the garden, "being in an agony, He prayed more earnestly," that was supplication. Supplication, therefore, goes beyond prayer, as being more earnest, more agonising, more vehement, more importunate, more breathed out with weeping and groaning. Thus the Lord says of His people, "They shall come with weeping, and with supplications will I lead them." To use a figure which I have before employed in one of my sermons, prayer is like a calm, deep river, which flows through a level country to the sea; but supplication resembles a mountain torrent, which rushes impetuously to the same ocean, but is broken with rocks strewed in its bed, which cannot stay, though they may impede its course. Each is of the Spirit, as the water of river and torrent is the same; and each is suitable to different circumstances

31

of the soul. But whether it be prayer or whether it be supplication, we are bidden here, "In everything by prayer and supplication to let our requests be made known unto God." The blessed Spirit in His various influences as a Spirit of grace and supplications in the hearts of God's people, to use another figure, may be compared to the wind. Sometimes it blows a scarcely perceptible breeze. The warm and gentle south wind on some days, falls upon our faces as fresh and sweet as if it had just passed over a bank of violets. So prayer sometimes in the soul is a gentle, warm aspiration heavenward, and yet, as being the breath of the Spirit, has in it a sweetness sensibly felt and a power that lifts up the heart into the presence of God. At another time the soul is cast into a very difficult position, lies under the pressure of a heavy affliction or is assailed by a grievous temptation; then prayer becomes more like the rushing, mighty wind which was heard on the day of Pentecost. If the gentle breeze of which I have just spoken speeds the ship of the soul gently over the wave, the more powerful breeze which I am now describing more resembles the strong wind that puts every sail of the vessel in motion, and bears her rapidly over the rough sea. But whether gentle breeze or strong gale, do not both bear her on to the same harbour? Sometimes again prayer may be mingled with tears and groans and sighs, just like a stormy day, when wind and rain seem to strive with each other for the mastery. This turns prayer into supplication; for, as I said before, supplication is stronger than prayer, more repeated, broken, continual, earnest, and more poured forth as if the answer must come immediately, or the soul could not live under the agonizing pressure of guilt and temptation.

But though I say this, I cannot help expressing my opinion how lamentably deficient are we here! How, under some temporal trial, you can go to a fellow sinner, and din his ear by telling him what a poor, afflicted creature you are, how sick in body, or how tried in circumstances, until you weary him and yourself with a thrice-told tale of misery and woe; and yet when you get home you have neither heart nor tongue to tell the same tale to God. Then

32

you wonder how it is that day by day you get no good, no relief, no help, no support. Here all of us, I may say, most lamentably fail for such is the desperate state of man by the fall, so careless is he and so prayerless, that nothing but the continual pouring out of a Spirit of grace and of supplications can move and enable the heart to act upon this comprehensive precept, "In everything by prayer and supplication with thanksgiving, let your requests be made known unto God."

We are often like Joash, who only smote on the ground three times with his arrows whereas Elisha said that if he had smitten five or six times then he would have utterly consumed Syria (See 2 Kings 13. 8,19).

During the pastorate of Daniel Matthews at Willenhall, there was an uneducated old man who had read the word importunate and did not understand what it meant. As he went to chapel that day he begged of the Lord to show him what it really meant. Part way through his sermon, Daniel Matthews said, "if you want to know what prayer is, it is knocking at the door of mercy". With that he gave a loud knock on the side of the pulpit. He then went on to say, "and if you want to know what importunate prayer is then it is this." At which he gave several knocks on the pulpit saying "Keep on knocking!" The old man had his answer.

The case of the imbecile lad, whose disease could not be healed by the disciples, illustrates forcibly this point. Our Lord's answer to the disciples' question, "Why could we not cast him out?" was "...Because of your unbelief; for verily I say unto you, If ye have faith as a grain of mustard seed, ye shall say unto this mountain, Remove hence to yonder place; and it shall remove and nothing shall be impossible unto you. Howbeit this kind cometh not out but by prayer and fasting" (Matthew 17. 20-21). One way of spiritual fasting is when we are so taken up with our case and need that all other things for the present must give way to that one desire.

How we need to take example from Elijah's command to his servant, "...Go again seven times" (1 Kings 18. 43). The cloudless sky, far from inhibiting Elijah only served under God to make him more importunate. "The effectual fervent prayer of a righteous man availeth much" (James 5. 16).

(9)   We do not need an answer yet.

It is an important lesson to learn, that God's delays are not always denials. Often, this path of waiting in prayer is the time of the trial of our faith. Abraham's long wait for the promised seed, Isaac, made the answer all the more precious and significant when it came.

"...for they shall not be ashamed that wait for Me" (Isaiah 49. 23).

How often we expect tomorrow's grace today! The Lord has said, "Take therefore no thought for the morrow: for the morrow shall take thought for the things of itself. Sufficient unto the day is the evil thereof" (Matthew 6. 34), and "...as thy days, so shall thy strength be" (Deuteronomy 33. 25). It is a great degree of faith when we are enabled to 'live a day at a time'. "Let your conversation be without covetousness; and be content with such things as ye have: for He hath said, I will never leave thee, nor forsake thee, so that we may boldly say, The Lord is my helper, and I will not fear what man shall do unto me" (Hebrews 13. 5-6).

Some years ago, a young teacher had the unenviable task of teaching mathematics to a class of fifteen year old children, who had no interest in school whatsoever, far less in mathematics. They had a bad reputation among the staff and no-one looked forward to teaching them as they were so disruptive. To this young teacher, the class became a great mountain, so much so that he would spend most of the week worrying about how the next lesson with these children would go. One Tuesday afternoon after a particularly harrowing time with this class, he being a praying man, laid the matter before the Lord as he had done many times before, that the Lord would help him in maintaining discipline and order. However his mind found no relief and instead he sunk into a state of deep anxiety about the next lesson which was not until Friday. It was the weeknight service, and in this state, he went to the chapel. The pastor, not knowing anything about this matter preached from the words, "Sufficient unto the day is the evil thereof" (Matthew 6.34). During this service the pastor emphasised the point that the Lord does not give grace for the day until the day arrives. This young man had been expecting Friday's grace on Tuesday evening! He went home in a different frame believing that prayer would be answered when the time came. With a mixture of fear and hope he entered the classroom on Friday afternoon, and to his amazement the class were like lambs. Indeed from that day on they were never so difficult. What a lesson this was for this young teacher, that God sends His answers when we need them but not before. Abraham said to Isaac, "My son, God will provide Himself a lamb for the burnt offering:" (Genesis 22. 8). They had to go on in faith that the prayer would be answered.

"Say not my soul, from whence can God relieve thy care,
Remember that Omnipotence hath servants everywhere.
His method is sublime, His thoughts supremely kind;
God never is before His time, and never is behind."

(10) We may already have an answer, but unbelief hides it from us.

How often, when Israel came into some fresh difficulties, they were prone to go to the Lord, almost as if He had never done anything for them before, whereas, His lovingkindness in times past, should have been ample assurance, even without fresh tokens, that He would not fail them, nor forsake them. "Delight thyself also in the Lord; and He shall give thee the desires of thine heart" (Psalm 37. 4).

Does not John Newton's complaint in his well known hymn below, show from his rich experience that the Lord was answering his prayers albeit in an unexpected way?

> "I asked the Lord that I might grow
> In faith, and love, and every grace;
> Might more of His salvation know,
> And seek more earnestly His face.
>
> 'Twas He who taught me thus to pray,
> And He, I trust, has answered prayer;
> But it has been in such a way
> As almost drove me to despair.
>
> 'Lord why is this?' I trembling cried;
> 'Wilt Thou pursue Thy worm to death?'
> 'Tis in this way,' the Lord replied,
> 'I answer prayer for grace and faith.'"

How Mary Magdalene, disappointed at the empty tomb, did not realise that its very emptiness was the answer to her deepest need. However when she turned and saw the Lord

Jesus and He, with the one word, 'Mary', dispelled her unbelief, she then saw 'light in God's light'.

The following extract from the life of Mr L.R.Broome as recorded in "Surely Goodness and Mercy" is a profitable example of this point.

"Very remarkably I had my future pathway revealed to me on Friday evening last and have now written to Southampton accepting D.V. the pastorate in 1940. After repeated attempts all the week, I was brought at last on Friday to give up all hope of defining my feelings or leadings to Mr Walley in a letter, and was writing to him to that effect. And then the words, 'Blind unbelief is sure to err,' came with such effect into my heart and showed me so clearly what I was doing that it quite broke me down. Then I believe I was enabled to take hold of the very blessed truth, 'God is His own interpreter, and He will make it plain'. The effect was such as to settle my mind in a moment. Several other things followed to confirm me, particularly the reading of Matthew Chapter 17, verses 14 -20. "

Again in this Extract from "In all Their Afflictions", by Murdoch Campbell we have another example of prayer answered in a different way from what is expected.

He writes: "A man I knew once stood up to pray. He was a man who lived very near the Lord but one who also passed through great spiritual conflicts. He had been purged like gold and sifted as wheat. 'Lord,' he said, 'some of us have, through the years, been praying for deeper holiness of life; but if we had known how our prayers were to be answered we might sometimes have withheld our voice.' It was, in other words, by 'fearful things' that the Lord answered his prayers. "

(11)   God has some better thing for us.

How often we are so dim in our perception of what we need as an answer to prayer! Often God has "...some better thing for us...".

It is often the case with God's dear people that "Disappointment proves to be His appointment" and they live to thank God for the denial of their prayer when they see what better thing God has in store. Jacob had to let Benjamin go, against his will, in order that he might hear the glad tidings, "...Joseph is yet alive..." (Genesis 46. 26).

How David longed to build a temple for the Lord and was encouraged by Nathan to proceed until he was sent back with an infinitely better answer than an earthly temple. The Lord promised that His dear Son would come of the seed of David and in this David saw by faith the temple of the Lord's body which infinitely outshone all that he had planned or that Solomon built later. No wonder David said to the Lord, "...Who am I, O Lord GOD? And what is my house, that Thou has brought me hitherto? And this was yet a small thing in Thy sight, O Lord GOD; but Thou has also spoken of Thy servant's house for a great while to come. And is this the manner of man, O Lord GOD? (2 Samuel 7. 18-20).

In Paul's case, the thorn was not removed, but he had the precious promise, "...My grace is sufficient for thee: for My strength is made perfect in weakness...." (2 Corinthians 12. 9).

In 1 Kings 19, Elijah prays that his life might be taken away, but the Lord had some better thing for him, namely, that he should not see death, but should be translated.

Pre-eminently, in the case of our Lord Jesus Christ, the cup which His Father gave Him was not taken from Him because, as Paul tells us:

"...who for the joy that was set before Him endured the cross, despising the shame, and is set down at the right hand of the throne of God" (Hebrews 12. 2).

There was a man named Roderick Macrae, in the North of Scotland, who lived at the beginning of the last century. He was known as a man of prayer and was a contemporary of Hugh Ross, Kilmuir. Although catechist of Creich, he was a man who feared that in his spiritual experience he had not enough law work. There is a tradition current to the effect that once when at a Communion season at Tain, he entered a clump of trees to find a quiet spot for his private devotions. There he began to bewail the unbroken nature of his heart, and, seizing two stones, he began to beat them together and to cry that his heart was as hard and unbreakable as they were. He pleaded that he might pass through deep conviction of sin lest that in the end he prove to be a hypocrite. Hugh Ross, who had also gone for the same purpose to a corner near him, overheard his bemoanings and petitions, and at once fell upon his knees and most earnestly sought that his friend's prayer might not be answered, for, said he, "if his prayer be answered he will go to splinters."

Also, William Gadsby at one time in his ministry thought that he needed a holiday, whereupon he arranged to go for a few days to Buxton. On the morning, that he was due to go, he fell down and broke his leg, and so was unable to go away as he had anticipated. In commenting on this event to a friend, he said, "My Master and I were both agreed that I needed a rest, but we were not of the same mind as to where it should be." Mr. Gadsby was so favoured in his soul at this time that he blessed God for thwarting his plans, proving that He had something better for him. Likewise God sometimes does not give us what we ask for but has something better in store.

(12)   Are we praying for the right things?

It is very important for us to recognise that whilst it is good and right for us to pray for providential blessings, yet we should never be content with anything less than spiritual blessings. How many are like the little boy who saw another boy who was blind with a dog. When he was asked what he would like most if he was blind like that little boy, he said that he would like a dog, whereas the best thing he could have asked was to receive his sight! How encouraging are the precious words in Luke 11. 11-13. "If a son shall ask bread of any of you that is a father, will he give him a stone? or if he ask a fish, will he for a fish give him a serpent? Or if he ask an egg, will he offer him a scorpion? If ye then being evil know how to give good gifts unto your children: how much more shall your heavenly Father give the Holy Spirit to them that ask Him?" How it honours God when we ask Him for all that He is so ready and willing to give to His children.

> "Thou art coming to a King;
> Large petitions with thee bring;
> For His grace and power are such,
> None can ever ask too much."   (John Newton)

What encouraging words Peter speaks to the lame man at the temple gate. "Silver and gold have I none; but such as I have give I thee: In the name of Jesus Christ of Nazareth rise up and walk" (Acts 3.6). Our God has indeed, the cattle upon a thousand hills and all the silver and the gold, but He has much more to give in the person and work of the Lord Jesus and the Holy Spirit!

Unanswered Prayer

The case of Monica, mother of Augustine of Hippo is another well known example of God having "some better thing for us."

In the year 354 A.D. a son was born into the family of a man named Patricius whose wife was Monica. The happy parents called him Augustine. They lived in North Africa, not very far from the ancient city of Carthage. Patricius was a pagan, but Monica was a fervent and sincere christian.

Patricius had great ambitions for his son. He soon saw that Augustine was very intelligent and so as soon as he thought his son could live independently he sent him to Carthage to finish his studies. Monica, however, who had higher thoughts for her son, sought to guide him towards the Word of God, and it was with a heavy heart that she left him in Carthage, where she knew that there were many temptations which would surround her son.

Her fears were only too soon realised, as Augustine became completely taken up with the social life in Carthage and it seemed that his mother's influence and prayers were thrown to the winds. All her warnings and entreaties fell on deaf ears. Augustine was determined to get "the most out of life," as he saw it.

Not far from where Monica lived, there was a godly bishop who encouraged her to keep praying for her son and he felt sure that her prayers concerning Augustine would one day be answered.

One of Monica's prayers was that her son would not leave Africa for Italy, because she feared that even greater temptations would face her rebellious son, than in Carthage. But this was a prayer which the Lord answered, by saying "no" to her request, for soon after he had finished his studies in Carthage, off Augustine went to Italy. It seems that his mother's worst fears were about to be realised! But, just as in the case of Joseph of old, "God meant it for good."

After spending some time in Rome, Augustine made his way to Milan, where in the providence of God he met a bishop named Ambrose, who became very interested in this young man.

Ambrose's sermons were used by the Holy Spirit to quicken the soul of Augustine, so that he began to study the Scriptures and as divine light entered his heart he began to understand the meaning of those two important words: sin and salvation. As he became convinced of his sin, Augustine passed through many days of darkness and temptation.

When he was thirty-one, still not having found forgiveness, he was in a garden in Milan, crying over his sins and asking for mercy. Whilst despairing of any hope, he suddenly heard the voice of a young child in a neighbouring garden, chanting, "Take and read; take and read." Without delay he turned to the Bible and opening on Romans 13. 13-14 he read the following words, "Let us walk honestly, as in the day; not in rioting and drunkenness, not in chambering and wantonness, not in strife and envying. But put ye on the Lord Jesus Christ and make not provision for the flesh to fulfil the lusts thereof." Almost at once divine light opened his heart to receive these words and he said all his doubts fled away. In his feelings, he passed from the sentence of death in his heart, to life in Christ Jesus.

His mother, who had followed him to Milan, was overjoyed to see her prayers answered at last and gave thanks to God for His mercy to her in saving her son by grace.

Although Augustine had become a teacher in Italy he now returned to Africa, seeking to live a quiet life in studying God's Word. He wrote one of the most famed of all books in the christian world, his Confessions, in which he describes the way he had been called by God's grace. He was soon appointed a bishop in a place called Hippo, in North Africa. From that time he became a leader of the Church of Christ, his influence spreading far and wide as he contended for the doctrines of grace.

Conclusion:

The mystery of prayer, its answers and its apparent disappointments is great and deep. The realisation that God is sovereign, and that we are unworthy of the least of His favours should be salutary reminders of our indebtedness to His goodness and mercy. That there should be such an avenue of mercy as prayer, and that there should be so many promises and instances of answers, display the absolute goodness of Almighty God to us.

Where faith is tried, and our prayers seem to go unanswered, may God give us the faith of Habakkuk who said, "Although the fig tree shall not blossom, neither shall fruit be in the vines; the labour of the olive shall fail, and the fields shall yield no meat; the flock shall be cut off from the fold, and there shall be no herd in the stalls: Yet I will rejoice in the LORD, I will joy in the God of my salvation. The LORD God is my strength, and He will make my feet like hinds' feet, and He will make me to walk upon mine high places..." (Habakkuk 3. 17-19).

In Hannah's pathway, we read of one to whom the problem of unanswered prayer was a real trial. It seemed that no one understood her case. Peninah provoked her, Elkanah misunderstood her and Eli rebuked her. How tenderly we should deal with those who may be walking in this path. Those of God's people who have had answers perhaps more quickly than others need especial grace to deal kindly with those who still wait or are having to face the humbling fact that the Lord is saying no to their petitions. Moses was given the grace to humble himself under the Lord's hand in this path and Aaron never showed greater grace than when he saw his own sons cut off before his very eyes.

One thing is absolutely certain. God's promise still stands as firm as ever, "...him that cometh to Me I will in no wise cast out" (John 6. 37).

"Be careful for nothing; but in every thing by prayer and supplication with thanksgiving let your requests be made known unto God. And the peace of God, which passeth all understanding, shall keep your hearts and minds through Christ Jesus" (Philippians 4. 6-7).

Come, my soul, thy suit prepare,
Jesus loves to answer prayer;
He Himself has bid thee pray,
Therefore will not say thee, Nay.

Thou art coming to a King;
Large petitions with thee bring;
For His grace and power are such,
None can ever ask too much.

With my burden I begin;
Lord, remove this load of sin;
Let Thy blood, for sinners spilt,
Set my conscience free from guilt.

While I am a pilgrim here,
Let Thy love my spirit cheer;
As my Guide, my Guard, my Friend,
Lead me to my journey's end.

Show me what I have to do;
Every hour my strength renew;
Let me live a life of faith;
Let me die Thy people's death   (John Newton)

Appendix

THOUGHTS ON PRAYER
by F. Windridge
in letters to his wife

1. Place

In writing on the subject of prayer, I do need God's gracious help in a special way, so that what I write shall be profitable to us both.

God has exhorted His dear people not to forsake the assembling of themselves together for worship, but He can hear prayer from any place; for He says: "From the rising of the sun even unto the going down of the same My name shall be great among the Gentiles; and in every place incense shall be offered unto My name, and a pure offering" (Malachi 1. 11). And Jesus said: "Woman, believe Me, the hour cometh, when ye shall neither in this mountain, nor yet at Jerusalem, worship the Father... God is a Spirit: and they that worship Him must worship Him in spirit and in truth" (John 4. 21, 24). So that the place *now* is of no importance; the frame of the heart is the thing.

We see from the Word of God that God has had dealings with sinners from a great variety of places since the beginning of the world. No doubt Noah prayed to God in the ark, and Jehoshaphat cried unto Him and was heard from the field of battle. Jacob prayed upon his bed; Jonah in the belly of the fish; the Ethiopian eunuch in a chariot; Daniel in the den of lions; Jeremiah in a dungeon; Israel in an enemy's land (Psalm 137. 1); the three Hebrews in a fiery furnace; Nathanael under a fig tree; Jonah under the gourd; Cornelius in the house; The Apostle John in the Isle of Patmos; Saul of Tarsus on a journey

(Acts 9. 5); Nehemiah in a king's palace (Nehemiah 1. 1); Elijah in a loft (1 Kings 17. 19) and on Mount Carmel; Gideon under an oak; Samson between the pillars; Peter on a roof-top (Acts 10. 9); Paul in a storm at sea (Acts 27. 23); the children of Israel in the street (Ezra 10. 9); David in a threshing-floor (2 Samuel 24. 24-25); the disciples in an upper room (Acts 1. 13-14); Abram in a valley (Genesis 14. 17, 22); Eliezer by a well (Genesis 24. 13).

"In all places where I record My name I will come unto thee, and I will bless thee" (Exodus 20. 24). How beautifully the words of the poet harmonize with all this!

> "Where'er they seek Thee, Thou art found,
> And every place is hallowed ground" (William Cowper)

2. Relationship, Condition and Occupation.

It is God's will and pleasure to pour out a spirit of prayer on all sorts of people----people of every possible relationship, condition of life, and occupation.

Relationship: "He shall turn the heart of the fathers to the children, and the heart of the children to their fathers" (Malachi 4. 6). He has sometimes blessed husband or wife as an instrument in the conversion of the other: "For what knowest thou, O wife! whether thou shalt save thy husband? or how knowest thou O man! whether thou shalt save thy wife?" (1 Corinthians 7. 16). Even Laban, not a godly man, said concerning Jacob: "I have learned by experience that the Lord hath blessed me for thy sake" (Genesis 30. 27), though the blessing was but temporal. But God has certainly used earthly relatives as a means of spiritual blessing to those

related to them, as the following instances appear to show:
Brother (John 1. 41), cousin (Esther 2. 7), daughter-in-law
(Ruth 1. 22), daughters (Acts 21. 9), father-in-law
(Exodus 18. 1), grandmother (2 Timothy 1. 5), husband
(Matthew 1. 19), mother (2 Timothy 1. 5), nephew
(Colossians 4. 10), sister (Exodus 15. 20), son (1 Kings 8. 12-
61), uncle (1 Chronicles 27. 32), widow (Ruth 1. 3), wife
(1 Samuel 25. 40).

Condition and Occupation: "God is mighty, and des-
piseth not any" (Job 36. 5). "Whosoever shall call upon the
name of the Lord shall be saved" (Romans 10. 13). And He
has enabled people of all ages and all sorts of occupations to
pray to Him, and has also answered their petitions. The
following are some that might be mentioned: Apothecary
(Nehemiah 3. 8), armourbearer (1 Samuel 14. 6-7), babes and
sucklings (Psalm 8. 2; Matthew 21. 16), beggar (Luke 16. 20),
centurion (Acts 10. 1-2), counsellor (Nehemiah 1. 11), deputy
(Acts 13. 7), eloquent man (Acts 18. 24), fisherman (Matthew
4. 18), governor (Genesis 45. 26), herdman (Amos 7. 14),
interpreter (Daniel 1. 17), jailer (Acts 16. 30), king (2 Samuel
7. 18), learned man (1 Corinthians 14. 18), little captive maid
(2 Kings 5. 2), master (Ruth 2. 4), mighty monarch
(Daneiel 4. 37), nobleman (John 4. 46), old disciple (Acts 21.
16), physician (Colossians. 4. 14), ploughman (1 Kings 19. 19),
publican (Luke 19. 8), rich man (Matthew 27. 57), scribe (Ezra
7. 6), seller of purple (Acts 16. 14), servant (Philemon 10),
soldiers (Luke 3. 14), tentmakers (Acts 18. 3), vinedresser
(Genesis 9. 20), wise men (Matthew 2. 1), young men and
maidens (Psalm 148. 12; 2 Chronicles 34. 1-3; 2 Timothy 3.
15; Genesis 24; Acts 12. 13).

The providential dealings of God with His people are often inseparable from His gracious dealings:

> "Sovereign Ruler of the skies,
> Ever gracious, ever wise;
> All my times are in Thy hand,
> All events at Thy command."   (John Ryland)

> "Grace and providence unite."   (Richard Burnham)

> "His skill infallible,
> His providential grace,
> His power and truth that never fail,
> Shall order all my ways."   (Charles Wesley)

> "Oh wondrous wheel of providence,
> Held in Jehovah's hand;
> Mysterious to the sons of sense,
> Moved by divine command!"   (David Denham)

3. *Some wonderful instances of God's power.*

There is no possible trial, sorrow, difficulty, or danger from which God cannot deliver such as pray to Him. He Himself asks the question: "Is anything too hard for the Lord?" (Genesis 18. 14).

He is the Maker of heaven and earth (Exodus 20. 11), has all the hearts of men in His hands (Psalm 33. 15), and can turn them whithersoever He will (Nehemiah 1. 11; Proverbs 21. 1). The whole creation is in His hand, and is called upon to praise Him (Psalm 148). Every part of it has been made to minister to the needs of His dear people. In fact, to vindicate His own

48

name and to defend and provide for His children, He has turned both heaven and earth "upside-down" (Isaiah 24. 1).

> "In heaven, and earth, and air, and seas,
> He executes His firm decrees." (Benjamin Beddome)

In answer to prayer He has sent one angel to destroy a powerful army of many thousands of men (Isaiah 37. 36), and on another occasion a mighty host of angels to protect one man (2 Kings 6. 17). He has made sun and moon to stand still for a whole day (Joshua 10. 12); stars in their courses to fight, possibly by withdrawing their light (Judges 5. 20); great hailstones to fall upon men (Exodus 9. 22; Joshua 10. 11); sent thunder and rain to terrify and teach the disobedient (1 Samuel 12. 17). He can raise a storm at sea to subdue a rebellious prophet (Jonah 1. 4), and another to show to the disciples His tender compassion and power in quelling it (Mark 4. 37-39); a cloud to make darkness to His enemies and to give light to His own people (Exodus 14. 20); yea, He has even turned back the sun in the heavens in answer to prayer (Isaiah 38. 8).

What wonders He has wrought in answer to the cries of His distressed children! Nothing is too small for His notice (Matthew 10. 30), or too great for His almighty power (Jeremiah 32. 17). He has caused His creatures again and again to act contrary to their nature. He has made an iron axe to swim (2 Kings 6. 6), and fish to die in the rivers (Exodus 7. 21). He has made men healthier and better looking on such simple food as lentils, than others who have been fed on the choicest meats (Daniel 1. 15). He has made the barren fruitful and the fruitful barren (1 Samuel 2. 5); weak women as bold as lions (1 Samuel 25. 20; 2 Samuel 20. 16), and strong men, even such as were bent on murder, to become as tender as women (Genesis 33. 4); lions to be as harmless as lambs (Daniel 6. 22), men to be stronger than lions (Judges 14. 6; 1 Samuel 17. 35), and swift as horses in the valleys or roes upon the mountains (1 Kings 18. 46; 1 Chronicles 12. 8); cruel birds of prey (Proverbs 30. 17) to take meat to feed a man (1 Kings 17. 6); the devouring element of fire to become as comfortable as a bed of roses without any thorns (Daniel 3. 25).

He has sent wind, earthquake and fire to destroy His enemies (Exodus 15. 10; Numbers 16. 32; 2 Kings 1. 10), and the same things to lead the way to a blessing upon His servant (1 Kings 19. 11-12). He has made waters to divide and stand upright and rigid as a wall (Exodus 14. 22), and mountains and hills to melt like wax (Judges 5. 5; Psalm 97. 5); a sinful man to walk upon the sea (Matthew 14. 29), and gallant ships to sink in it (2 Chronicles 20. 37); a lump of figs to cure a boil (2 Kings 20. 7), and a serpent of brass to heal a serpent bite (Numbers 21. 9); an angel to cook meals for a man (1 Kings 19. 6), and a man to prepare a meal for angels (Genesis 18. 8; Hebrews 13. 2); a dried-up stick to bring forth fruit (Numbers 17. 8), a fig tree to wither away in a night (Mark 11. 20), and a gourd to come up suddenly and to perish as quickly (Jonah. 4. 10); a man to become dumb (Luke 1. 20), and a dumb ass to speak (Numbers 22. 28; 2 Peter 2. 16); a man at one time to carry a tremendous weight up a hill, and afterwards to become as weak as any other man (Judges 16. 3, 21).

God can make a man forget a most important dream, and reveal to another man both the dream and its interpretation (Daniel 2.). He can cause the solitary fingers of a man's hand to write a message on a wall (Daniel 5. 5), and the bones of a buried prophet to bring another dead man to life (2 Kings 13. 21). He can reveal to an ass the presence of an angel, and hide that angel from the person riding on the ass (Numbers 22. 27, 31). He can show to His servants the glorified spirits of two men (Luke 9. 30), and He can also conceal from the keen eyes of Satan the place where the body of one of them is buried (Deuteronomy 34. 6; Jude 9). God can hide a man from all the spies sent forth by a king (1 Kings 18. 10), and conceal another from his brethren even when they are talking with him (Genesis 42. 8). He can also reveal to a man what an enemy king says in his bedroom (2 Kings 6. 12), send an angel from heaven to give a praying man the name and address of a Gospel minister (Acts. 10. 5-6), and even let men hear what people in heaven are talking about (Luke 9. 30). He can make it impossible for a whole army to capture one man (I Samuel 23. 14), and also make it possible for one man, single-handed and without carnal weapons, to capture a whole army (2 Kings 6. 18). To save His people He has caused their enemies to destroy one another (2 Chronicles 20. 23), to imagine that they see dreadful sights (2 Kings 3. 22), hear strange and war-like noises, and to flee from non-existent armies (2 Kings 7. 6; 19. 7).

Yet He can also deliver by the simplest means --- a butler (Genesis 41. 9), a bone (Judges 15. 15, 19), a bolster (1 Samuel 19. 16), a black man (Jeremiah 38. 12-13), or a basket (Acts 9. 25). He can cause a man to read for the first time a message from a prophet who has already been seven years in heaven (2 Chronicles 21. 12); and He can, *also for the first time*, let a prophecy appear in His written Word three thousand years after it was uttered (Jude 14, 15).

To enable a man to pay a vow, God can cause a fish to vomit him out on the dry land (Jonah 2. 10); and to enable others to pay tribute unto Caesar, He can cause another fish to yield up half-a-crown (Matthew 17. 27).

51

"He ravens and lions can tame!
All creatures obey His commands!
Then let us rejoice in His name,
And leave all our cares in His hands." (John Newton)

It may be that you will say that all these things are very wonderful, but they do not seem to touch us in our ordinary life. But they are proofs of the power of God, and of His care for His dear people.

"There's not a sparrow, nor a worm,
But's found in God's decrees." (Isaac Watts)

5. *The Pardon of Sin.*

I have spoken of many temporal things asked for and received, but have said little about spiritual blessings prayed for. Among these, surely the pardon of sin is one of the greatest.

"If sin be pardoned, I'm secure;
Death has no sting beside." (Isaac Watts)

I know, and painfully feel from day to day, that I am a sinner. I need pardon; and in the Word of God are many encouragements to ask for pardon, as well as for other blessings. Oftentimes we feel we cannot pray; but God graciously describes as prayer many feelings which we scarcely believe to be prayer.

To Solomon God said, "*Ask* what I shall give thee" (1 Kings 3. 5). To Israel, Malachi says: "And now, I pray you, *beseech*

God that He will be gracious unto us" (Malachi 1. 9). Jeremiah speaks of *breathing* as being prayer (Lamentations 3. 56). By Jeremiah also the Lord speaks thus; "*Call* unto Me, and I will answer thee, and show thee great and mighty things, which thou knowest not" (Jeremiah 33. 3). Hezekiah had such a low opinion of his prayer that he said, "Like a crane or a swallow, so did I *chatter*" (Isaiah 38. 14). David says: "Hear my *cry*, O God! attend unto my prayer" (Psalm. 61. 1). Again: "He will fulfil the *desire* of them that fear Him" (Psalm 145. 19).

In true prayer there is something of expectation, and we read that "the expectation of the poor shall not perish for ever" (Psalm 9. 18). Prayer is further described as "having fled for refuge" (Hebrews 6. 18). And how glad I have been to read that God does "hear the *groaning* of the prisoner", and will "loose those that are appointed to death" (Psalm 102. 20). "The Lord looketh on the heart" (1 Samuel 16. 7). His eyes "run to and fro throughout the whole earth, to shew Himself strong in the behalf of them whose heart is perfect toward Him" (2 Chronicles 16. 9). Josiah is particularly pointed out and blessed "because his heart was tender" in prayer (2 Chronicles 34. 27). Manasseh was said to *intreat* God in his prayer, humbling himself greatly (2 Chronicles 33. 19). Prayer is described also as *knocking* (Matthew 7. 7), *longing* (Psalm 107. 9), *looking* (Psalm 34. 5), *mourning* (Matthew 5. 4), feeling a *need* (Psalm 9. 18), making a *noise* (Psalm 55. 2), *petitioning* (Psalm 20. 5), *requesting* (Psalm 21. 2), *seeking* (Lamentations 3. 25), *shouting* (Lamentations 3. 8), *sighing* (Psalm 12. 5), *striving* (Luke 13. 24), *supplicating* (Psalm 6. 9), *trembling* at God's Word (Isaiah 66. 2), *vowing* (Psalm 132. 2), *waiting* (Proverbs 20. 22), *weeping* (Psalm 6. 8), *wrestling* (Genesis 32. 24). If we cannot wrestle, surely we long, desire, feel a need.

"The sinner born of God,
To God will pour his prayer,
In sighs, or groans, or words expressed,
Or in a falling tear.

The feelings of his heart
Ascend to the Most High;
And though the Lord awhile forbear,
His needs He will supply." (William Gadsby)

Some Objections Answered

I know that none but the Lord Himself can deliver us from all the hindrances to prayer, and by putting forth His power answer all our objections. Oh that He would condescend to bless His own Word, as I now quote from it in reply to some of the objections that arise now and then in my own mind!

I fear I am too sinful to receive pardon. "All manner of sin and blasphemy shall be forgiven unto men" (Matthew 12. 31). Paul was "before a blasphemer, and a persecutor and injurious;" but he obtained mercy, because he did it ignorantly in unbelief (I Timothy 1. 13). Seven devils were cast out of Mary Magdalene (Mark 16. 9).

I fear my sins are too many. "Let him return unto the Lord, and He will have mercy upon him; and to our God, for He will abundantly pardon" (Isaiah 55. 7). "Thou wilt cast all their sins into the depths of the sea" (Micah 7. 19).

My sins have been of such a daring character that they have reached the very heavens. "Thy mercy is great above the heavens"(Psalm 108. 4). "As the heaven is high above the earth, so great is His mercy toward them that fear Him" (Psalm 103. 11).

54

Is it possible that God can ever forget the wickedness I have committed? "I will forgive their iniquity, and I will remember their sin no more" (Jeremiah 31. 34; Hebrews 8. 12).

My sins have been so base, mean, degrading, loathsome. "Underneath are the everlasting arms" (Deuteronomy 33. 27). "God hath chosen... base things of the world" (1 Corinthians 1. 27, 28). "Such were some of you; but ye are washed" (1 Corinthians 6. 11).

I have treacherously departed from God after many sweet favours and many hopes of being faithful. "Thou hast played the harlot with many lovers; yet return again to Me, saith the Lord" (Jeremiah 3. 1).

My sins are like a great mountain. "Who art thou, O great mountain? before Zerubbabel thou shalt become a plain" (Zechariah 4. 7). "If ye have faith as a grain of mustard seed, ye shall say unto this mountain, Remove hence to yonder place, and it shall remove; and nothing shall be impossible unto you" (Matthew 17. 20).

I am so far away from God. "They shall remember Me in far countries" (Zechariah 10. 9). "But now in Christ Jesus, ye who sometimes were far off are made nigh by the blood of Christ" (Ephesians 2. 13). "As far as the east is from the west, so far hath He removed our transgressions from us" (Psalm 103. 12). "When he was yet a great way off his father saw him, and had compassion, and ran, and fell on his neck, and kissed him" (Luke 15. 20).

I feel altogether prayerless. "I will pour upon the house of David, and upon the inhabitants of Jerusalem, the spirit of grace and supplications" (Zechariah 12. 10).

I am so hard. "God maketh my heart soft" (Job 23. 16). "I will be as the dew unto Israel" (Hosea 4. 5).

My heart seems taken up with idols. "From all your idols, will I cleanse you" (Ezekiel 36. 25).

I am bound hand and foot as though in iron. Jesus is anointed "to proclaim liberty to the captives, and the opening of the prison to them that are bound" (Isaiah 61. 1).

I have a dreadfully sinful nature. "He will subdue our iniquities..." (Micah 7. 19).

Sin masters me. "Sin shall not have dominion over you" (Romans 6. 14).

I am very ignorant. "I will instruct thee and teach thee in the way which thou shalt go" (Psalm 32. 8).

I am blind. "I will bring the blind by a way that they knew not; I will lead them in paths that they have not known" (Isaiah 42. 16).

I feel deaf to God's Word. "The ears of the deaf shall be unstopped" (Isaiah 35. 5) .

I know not how to pray. "We know not what we should pray for as we ought: but the Spirit itself maketh intercession for us with groanings which cannot be uttered" (Romans 8. 26).

I feel nothing but an outcast. "He gathereth together the outcasts of Israel" (Psalm 147. 2).

I am but a stranger among God's people. "Moreover concerning a stranger, that is not of Thy people Israel, but cometh out of a far country for Thy name's sake;...when he shall come and pray toward this house; Hear Thou in heaven Thy dwelling place, and do according to all that the stranger calleth to Thee for" (1 Kings 8. 41-43).

I fear there is no room for me. "Lord, it is done as thou hast commanded, and yet there is room" (Luke14. 22).

My whole life seems to have been nothing but sin. "As for the wickedness of the wicked, he shall not fall thereby in the day that he turneth from his wickedness" (Ezekiel 33. 12).

What can I say? "Take with you words, and turn to the Lord; say unto Him, Take away all iniquity, and receive us graciously" (Hosea 14. 2).

I might continue with many more objections. All the Scriptures are well known and you say: "I want to feel the power; without that it is only the letter of Scripture". That is it --- power. Unless God, in infinite compassion, puts forth His sovereign and invincible power, we are indeed helpless. At the same time, I feel that shame and confusion of face belong to me for my neglect of the throne of grace. Oh that God would condescend to regard us in our low estate, and pour out upon us that great blessing of a spirit of prayer!

6. *The Foundation and Ground of Prayer.*

The first thought that occurs to me is: "Oh that God would so bless me in prayer, that I might be able from sweet experience to recommend prayer to you!" I painfully feel my destitution and the lack of a spirit of prayer. God only can give it, I know. I also feel my inability to deal with the subject; yet there is a sort of constraint upon me to make the attempt, and a feeble, very feeble desire that God will condescend to help me, and make the meditation profitable.

When our first parents fell from God, there could be no such thing as prayer on the footing of that covenant under which they were created. They were lost; God's favour was gone; and all that man could do was to get farther away from Him, which both of them tried to do. But God was determined to save some of the human race, and so the plan of salvation was revealed. The eternal Son of God engages to take man's nature, to obey in that nature the law of God, and

57

to suffer in that nature the curse due to His chosen. The Holy Spirit engages to bring every vessel of mercy to feel his need, and from that felt need to pray. But prayer must be put up in the name of Jesus, and though many of God's dear people do not at first realise it, their prayers for pardon would never be answered if Jesus had not died for them.

> "If sin be pardoned, I'm secure;
> Death has no sting beside."　　　(Isaac Watts)

Many sin-bitten souls can say this before they can understand that

> "The law gives sin its damning power;"　　(Isaac Watts)

and may know this third line for years before they can say,

> "But Christ my ransom died."　　　(Isaac Watts)

When God gave the law on Mount Sinai,

> "The law was never meant to give
> New strength to man's lost race;
> We cannot act before we live,
> And life proceeds from grace."　　(Joseph Hart)

It seems quite a natural question, "Why should God give a law, if man could not obey it?" That question is anticipated by Paul: "Wherefore then serveth the law?" And he answers it: "It was added because of transgressions, till the Seed (Christ) should come to whom the promise was made" (Galatians 3.19).

"That law but makes your guilt abound;
Sad help! and (what is worst)
All souls that under that are found,
By God Himself are cursed."   (Joseph Hart)

"By the law is the knowledge of sin" (Romans 3. 20). When a sinner is thoroughly tired out with the law, he is at last obliged to turn away from all vain attempts to keep it, and thus to fly to Christ, the Law-fulfiller.

It is most instructive to notice the mention of *blood* at the giving of the law on Mount Sinai (Exodus 24. 6). We might reasonably ask, "Why is blood mentioned at all? The people promise to obey the law; why bring in blood?" Because God knew they would not and could not obey, and the blood was to remind His own people among the national Israel that they needed an atonement, a sacrifice. The people said, "All that the Lord hath said will we do, and be obedient". God knew that they would break their promise, as we have ourselves personally done; and so even on the first occasion of writing the two tables, He makes provision for the transgressor. Chapters 25 to 31 are filled with an account of this provision for the law-breaker: the ark, the mercy-seat, the table, the candlestick, the tabernacle, the altar, the oil, the priests and their garments, the sacrifices, the incense, and so on, all setting forth in various ways the Lord Jesus Christ as the One grand and glorious way to God. While Moses is being instructed in all this, the people turn to idolatry of the most gross and revolting character, as recorded in chapter 32. But as was said before, God was not taken by surprise. He had already made provision for it, not only in the covenant of grace before time, but also in the things revealed in those preceding chapters.

59

By breaking the first commandment, Israel had broken the whole law (James 2. 10). When God wrote the law a second time, the two tables were put into the ark, which represented Christ; and they were never broken by Him, for He magnified the law and made it honourable (Isaiah 42. 21). Through Him therefore there is access to God.

> "I can have no access to God,
> But through the merits of His blood." (John Berridge)

He Himself says, "I am the way, the truth, and the life". On the mount of transfiguration the Father said: "This is My beloved Son, in whom I am well pleased; hear ye Him."

OTHER BOOKS AVAILABLE

Mary Jones and Her Bible
A compelling story of a young Welsh girl's thirst for the Truth and her determination to obtain a Bible in her own Language.

Bible doctrines Simply Explained: by B.A.Ramsbottom
A simple yet precious explanation of the vital doctrines of salvation in a manner suitable for all ages. Many lessons are drawn from experiences from every day life.

The Vital Year: by H.Salkeld
An enthralling account of a year in the author's life, in which he served in the trenches during the first World war. Throughout, the narrative is interspersed with spiritual lessons learned by the author, which made it to him "The Vital Year" of salvation in his soul.

The Things Most Surely Believed Among Us: by William Gadsby
A simple catechism for the instruction of all ages in the Truth. Well supported by Scripture references.

The Old is Better - Some Bible Versions Considered: by A.J.Levell
The author defends the Authorised Version as the best and most trustworthy version of the Bible in the English language. Written in layman's terms to help the reader get a basic understanding of how we got our Bible.

Spirit of Truth - Some Aspects of Charismatic Teaching:by J.R.Broome
The question is examined of how far such gifts of the Holy Spirit as tongues, healing, miracles and prophecy exist in the church today.

Published monthly is the *The Gospel Standard*, one of the oldest periodicals, contending for the doctrines of sovereign grace, the experience of believers and practice as revealed in the Word of God.
Also *The Friendly Companion*, a monthly magazine for children and young people setting forth the truths of the word of God

For a full list of titles please write to:
Gospel Standard Trust Publications
12(b) Roundwood Lane, Harpenden, Herts, AL5 3DD